Written by
Simon James Green
Illustrated by
Irma Ruggiero

Hachette UK's policy is to use papers that are natural, renewable and recyclable products and made from wood grown in sustainable forests and other controlled sources. The logging and manufacturing processes are expected to conform to the environmental regulations of the country of origin.

ISBN: 978 1 0360 0059 2

Text © Simon James Green
Design, illustrations and layout © 2025 Hodder & Stoughton Limited

First published in 2025 by Hachette Learning,
An Hachette UK Company
Carmelite House, 50 Victoria Embankment, London EC4Y 0DZ
www.HachetteLearning.com
The authorised representative in the EEA is Hachette Ireland, 8 Castlecourt Centre, Dublin 15, D15 XTP3, Ireland (email: info@hbgi.ie)

Impression number 10 9 8 7 6 5 4 3 2 1
Year 2029 2028 2027 2026 2025
Author: Simon James Green
Series Editor: Catherine Coe
Illustrator: Irma Ruggiero / Astound
Educational Consultant: Pauline Allen
Design layout: Lorraine Inglis

With thanks to the schools that took part in the development of Reading Planet *Cosmos*, including: Ancaster CE Primary School, Ancaster; Downsway Primary School, Reading; Ferry Lane Primary School, London; Foxborough Primary School, Slough; Griffin Park Primary School, Blackburn; St Barnabas CE First & Middle School, Pershore; Tranmoor Primary School, Doncaster; and Wilton CE Primary School, Wilton.

The Publishers would like to thank the following for permission to reproduce copyright material.
Cover and internal design (confetti): © Kristina Jalabi/stock.adobe.com.

All rights reserved. Apart from any use permitted under UK copyright law, no part of this publication may be reproduced or transmitted in any form or by any means, electronic or mechanical, including photocopying and recording, or held within any information storage and retrieval system, without permission in writing from the publisher or under licence from the Copyright Licensing Agency Limited. Further details of such licences (for reprographic reproduction) may be obtained from the Copyright Licensing Agency Limited, www.cla.co.uk

A catalogue record for this title is available from the British Library.

Printed in the UK.

To order please visit www.HachetteLearning.com or contact Customer Service at education@hachette.co.uk / +44 (0)1235 827827

Contents

1   Worst Idea Ever! 4

2   Cupid 14

3   How (not) to Make Hummus! . . 22

4   Return of the Hummus 30

5   Mmm ... Chocolate Cake! 35

6   Another Fine Mess! 43

7   Yay for Uncle Charlie! 50

8   Stinking Donkey 57

9   A Wedding to Remember! 64

10   Game on! 70

1 Worst Idea Ever!

Out of all of Mum's ideas, this one was the worst yet.

Not just the worst — actually horrific.

She wanted me to be a pageboy at her wedding.

I had two problems with this idea. First of all, this was the kind of job that little kids usually did, and I was eleven. I was *way* too mature. The second problem was even worse. She wanted me to bring the wedding ring down the aisle dressed up as Cupid, wearing a Roman-style toga complete with feathered wings and glitter boots.

When she told me, I thought it was so funny, I laughed for ten whole minutes.

And then I realised she wasn't joking.

I was already pretty much the least cool kid in Year 6. If any photos of me dressed as Cupid got out, my life would be over.

But Mum was insistent because it was her 'special day' and therefore I had to do whatever she wanted.

So, pretty much like any normal day then, am I right?!

Mum got divorced from my dad last year, and six months later she got engaged to Adamma, who she met at hot yoga, and long story short, now I was going to have two mums. Three, actually, if you include Kelly, who Dad is going to marry next year. So many mums. Mother's Day is going to bankrupt me, that's for sure.

Adamma also had a kid my age, and the only good thing about this whole embarrassing Cupid plan was that Henry was going to be a pageboy too, and he would be carrying the other ring down the aisle.

Henry lived with Adamma in their house across town, and I lived with Mum. Our mums were planning to sell their houses and buy one big house for us all to live in together after the wedding. I was a bit nervous about that. I was used to it just being me and Mum. What if Henry liked a different type of biscuit? Would we have to change brands? Where would his toothbrush go? Henry and I had spent some time together, but I just felt like I didn't know him well enough to be sure he wasn't about to wreck my very nice life with Mum.

One thing I *was* pretty sure about though was that he would feel the same as me about this Cupid nonsense. So hopefully we'd just get through it together, maybe have a bit of a laugh ... and then delete the photos, destroy the evidence, and pretend none of it ever happened.

Oh, how wrong I was.

It was a regular Wednesday night, exactly ten days before the wedding, when the trouble really started. The previous day, Henry had suggested it would be

a 'nice gesture' if we both bought a 'funny card' for our mums, congratulating them on the upcoming wedding. Fair enough, it seemed like a good thing to do, and hey, you never knew, maybe they'd be so pleased they'd change their minds about the Cupid thing and just let us wear normal suits instead. It had to be worth a go.

I was really pleased with the card I picked. I felt confident they would find it hilarious because I'm a funny guy and I know a thing or two about jokes. Here's one now:

Get it?!

The *kid ... napping* at school?

He *woke up*?

I mean, I should have my own show, or something.

Anyway, Adamma and Henry had come round for the evening, and Henry presented his card first, as we settled down in the lounge after dinner. Mum ripped open the envelope and pulled it out. It was a picture of two pears with cartoon faces, and a caption that read: 'You are *pear*-fect for each other!'

"Oh, Henry!" Mum said, smiling. "That's so cute and funny!"

I grimaced, because I wasn't sure it really was that funny, but OK, we all have a different sense of humour.

"Open it!" Henry said. "I've written a poem inside."

Mum opened the card and looked at the poem with a gentle smile on her face, like it was the most beautiful thing she'd ever read. "Roses are red, violets are blue, you love each other, and I love you." Mum had tears in her eyes. "Oh, Henry! That's so beautiful!" She looked at Adamma, who also had tears in her eyes. "What a kind, sensitive boy you are!"

"Thank you, that means a lot," Henry said, putting a hand on his heart. "Next week's wedding is going to be really special. I'm just so honoured to be a part of it."

I took a deep breath. It occurred to me Henry was taking this whole wedding thing a lot more seriously than me. Not only that, but he also seemed to be really impressing my mum, who was currently looking at him with hearts in her eyes, like he was the golden boy.

I'd been an only child for eleven whole years. I didn't mind the idea of a sibling, but no way was he going to take my place as Mum's favourite. Was that what he'd been planning, by suggesting the cards?

Was he trying to prove that he was somehow ... better than me? Kinder? More thoughtful? You know, all the qualities grownups really *love*?

Was this all part of his plan to make sure our mums bought the biscuits he liked?!

Anyway, it was fine because as I presented my card, I felt sure I was about to lighten the icky lovey-dovey mood with a bit of genuine comedy.

Everyone loves a comedian.

"There are three rings of marriage," Mum said, reading the words on the front of my card. "The engagement ring, the wedding ring ... and the bickering."

I waited for the laughter.

After a lot of silence, Mum eventually looked up at me. "Why would you choose this card, Max?"

"It's ... a joke!" I said, still waiting for the applause I so richly deserved.

Henry cleared his throat. "If two people love each other, they can usually work out their differences without bickering."

"Thank you, Henry, I agree," Mum said. "Never mind, I expect Max was just trying to be funny, weren't you?"

I held out my hands because, *er, yes!*

"Let's see what you've written inside ..." Mum continued.

"No, let's not!" I said, snatching the card off her.

"Give it back!" Mum said. "I'd like to see!"

"It doesn't matter now," I said, in a tug-of-war with the card and my mum. I felt like everything was starting to go wrong and nobody appreciated my sense of humour. "Just let me—"

The card ripped in half, leaving Mum with the side I'd written on. She glanced down at the words. "Roses are red, violets are blue, the dog is my favourite, but you're OK too." Mum blew out a breath. "Wow. I'm flattered."

"You don't even have a dog," Henry pointed out.

"It's. A. Joke!" I said.

"Well, it doesn't make sense," he replied. He smiled at my mum. "Roses are red, violets are blue, I'm lucky to have ... a second mum like you!"

"Oh, Henry! Did you make that up on the spot? You're so clever!" Mum cooed.

My eyes widened. He *was* trying to make my mum like him more than me! I bet he wanted his toothbrush in prime position in the pot, and mine ... probably on the floor! I wasn't going to let him get away with that! And if he wanted to make up poetry on the spot, two could play at that game! "Roses are red, violets are blue, your face is so pretty—" I stuttered to a halt, Mum looking at me expectantly, wondering what the end of the poem would be.

"My face is so pretty ... *what*?" Mum asked.

"It belongs in a zoo?" I suggested, unable to think of anything else that rhymed with 'blue'.

"Right, go to your room!" Mum told me.

"Oh, come on!"

"NOW!"

I sighed, bowed my head and left the room, but not before glancing at Henry and seeing the smug little smile on his lips.

So, this really was a battle then?

Fine!

One-nil to Henry.

But this wasn't over.

It had only just begun.

2 Cupid

On Friday, Mum took us both to try on our Cupid outfits while Adamma began preparations for the 'hen party' they were organising for the next day. Apparently a 'hen party' is when a bunch of the bride's mates all get together to celebrate the upcoming wedding. Some brides had a weekend at a hotel, or a trip to a big city, but Mum and Adamma had decided to keep their hen party more low-key. They'd just invited a few of their closest friends round to our house for food and drinks. Since I seriously needed to make up for my card yesterday, this had given me an excellent idea!

"I was thinking," I said, as Mum drove us over to the fancy-dress shop, "why don't I bake a nice cake for your hen party? I could do my famous chocolate cake — it's always a hit!"

This was absolutely true. I'd perfected my cake recipe over a couple of years, adding delicious jam and fresh cream to make it even more luxurious.

I'd made it for Mum's birthday last year, and she loved it so much, she asked me to make it for pretty much any celebration now.

"That would be lovely, Max!" Mum replied. "Adamma and I would love that — it's very sweet of you."

"No worries." I shrugged, glancing at Henry who was sitting next to me in the back seat. "*It would be an honour.*"

Now it was definitely one-all in the race to be the best kid ... or, at least, it was until Henry piped up a few moments later.

"I'd be *honoured* to make something too!" he announced. "How about some elderflower fizz for everyone to enjoy on arrival?"

"Ooh, elderflower fizz!" Mum cooed. "That sounds divine!"

I gritted my teeth. "Well, hang on, hang on!" I said. "I'll also get some passion-fruit fizz, in case any of your guests don't like elderflower — which I'm sure they won't!" I shot a poisoned look at Henry who rolled his eyes at me.

"I love the sound of both!" Mum said, keeping her eyes on the road.

"I'll do some nibbles too!" Henry said.

I took a deep breath and tried not to squeal.

"Do your friends like goat's cheese?" Henry continued.

Goat's cheese? What was he, some award-winning chef?!

"We all love goat's cheese," Mum said.

"Actually, I was going to do some nibbles as well!" I said, desperate to keep up. "It was totally on my list of things I'd love to contribute to your wedding. So, I was thinking … dips? Perhaps some hummus?"

"Will you be making the hummus yourself?" Henry asked. "Or will you just be buying it from a supermarket?"

I narrowed my eyes at him. "I'll be making it myself, naturally!"

Henry raised his eyebrows. "Do you know the recipe?"

"Yes, thank you, I do know the recipe! So, Mum, what—"

"What recipe will you be using?" Henry interrupted.

I chewed my lip. I had no idea how to make hummus. "It's my secret recipe," I told him. "But it's the most delicious hummus anyone will ever taste!"

"Is that so?" Henry said, with an arched eyebrow. "Can't wait to try it!"

"Can't wait to try your goat's cheese!" I snapped back. "Hope it won't taste like old socks!"

"Boys, boys!" Mum said. "All of these things sound lovely, so there's no need to argue."

"No one's arguing!" Henry chirped. "Max and I are best buddies! We're just super keen to make your wedding the best ever!"

"That's right!" I added.

We drove on for a bit, before Henry added, "Oh, by the way, I know Mum was really keen to have some nice music playing at the reception after the wedding. So I asked some friends who all play instruments, and they've agreed to form a string quartet and perform Mozart for us."

"Oh, Henry!" Mum said. "You really have gone the extra mile!"

"It's nothing," Henry said. "I'd do anything to make you both happy!"

Henry turned to me and gave me an evil smile and I did my best to stifle a scream of frustration. Whatever I did, Henry seemed to be one step ahead of me.

As we got out of the car and walked to the fancy-dress shop, I realised that I was going to have to up my game. I needed to go big and really impress everyone with something amazing and awe-inspiring.

But what could it be?

As we were being measured for our togas, it suddenly hit me. Mum loved horses! They were her favourite animal — she often talked of moving to the country and owning her own horse one day. I needed to involve a horse in this wedding — it would totally make her day. And now, I had the perfect idea!

"Mum?" I said, smiling. "I've been thinking about how we actually bring these rings to you during the wedding ceremony."

"We just walk down the aisle with them, don't we?" Henry said, adjusting his toga in the mirror opposite us.

"Well, we *could*," I said, "if we wanted to just be ordinary and boring. But actually, because it's such a special and important moment, I've decided to do something a bit different ..."

Henry crossed his arms over his chest, clearly worried.

"Mm? What had you in mind, Max?" Mum said, adjusting my toga. "I think it needs taking in a bit."

"Don't fret about the toga, Mum!" I said. "Cos this Cupid is going to be arriving down the aisle ... on horseback!"

Mum gasped.

Henry nearly choked on his own tongue.

Oh, yeah! This was the wedding stunt to end them all! No way would Henry be able to compete with this! I was going to wow the whole crowd and completely make it the best day ever for Mum and Adamma. I would be their Number One Kid for the rest of time!

Never mind getting to pick the household biscuits, I'd probably get some kind of award for this — you know, the ones they give children who have done extraordinary things! Maybe I'd get to be on telly, meet someone famous and then be given a prize for being brilliant — maybe a trip to Disneyland, or, at the very least, some new trainers.

"Max!" Mum said. "That sounds amazing!"

I grinned. "Yep! Uh huh!"

"What sort of horse and where will you get it from?!" she continued.

"Yep! Uh huh!" I said, still smiling.

"No, *what sort of horse and where will you get it from*?" Mum said again.

I ran my tongue over my lips. OK, sure, at the present time, there was no horse. But how hard could it be to get one? There were loads of horses in the world — surely someone would be kind enough to lend me one?

"Big horse," I said. "Really big horse. *Silver.*"

Mum gasped. "My favourite colour!"

"Yep! Uh huh!" I said, with a fixed grin. "I know a ... guy. With a horse."

"You can't even ride horses though, can you?" Mum said, frowning.

I cleared my throat. That was also true, but ... how hard could it be? I'd just have a quick lesson. It looked pretty easy on TV. And then everyone would gasp and coo as I majestically rode down the aisle on the back of a big silver horse and presented one of the rings to Mum ... while Henry just walked down the aisle and handed his to Adamma because he hadn't bothered to think of anything impressive.

"We wanted this wedding to be memorable," Mum said, "and that's exactly what it's going to be!"

I nodded. "Oh, it'll be memorable, all right! Everyone is going to remember this wedding!"

I turned to Henry and gave him an evil smile.

3 How (not) to Make Hummus!

It was the day of the hen party, but my mind wasn't really on all the preparations I was supposed to be doing. Apparently, no one was prepared to lend me a horse. It was completely outrageous. I'd asked everyone I knew and even been through the entire internet, but everyone had excuses as to why I wasn't allowed to borrow one of their horses. One woman told me I was 'too inexperienced', another said something about 'insurance' and a third just laughed down the phone. It was a total nightmare, but I couldn't give up. I'd promised Mum a horse at the wedding, and a horse she would have! Besides, I couldn't stand to think about the smug look on Henry's face if I didn't manage to pull it off. He'd never let me forget it.

Henry was busy doing something very delicate with goat's cheese on the kitchen work surface, so I stood at the table to make my chocolate cake. I was still thinking about how to get hold of a horse. I grabbed

some flour, sugar and cocoa. *I couldn't let Mum down!* I weighed my ingredients. *I had to somehow get a horse!* I mixed everything together in a big bowl.

But … wait a minute! Sometimes when you made cake, you could substitute one ingredient for a different one. For example, if you wanted the cake to be vegan, you could take out the butter and eggs and use vegetable oil instead.

What I needed to find was a substitute for the horse. It needed to be *like* a horse, but not an actual horse, since everyone was too mean to lend me one.

And I had just the creature in mind!

I quickly scraped my mixture into two baking tins, slammed them in the oven and hurried back to the computer, where I typed 'donkey sanctuary' into the search bar. I found a phone number for Hillgate Donkey Sanctuary, just a few miles away. Mr Hillgate at the sanctuary agreed to lend me a donkey called Brian. In exchange, I had to do a fundraising event at school for the sanctuary and muck out the stables every Saturday for a month. *Fine.* The deal was done. Brian the Donkey would be delivered to me outside the wedding venue just before I was due to parade down the aisle with the ring. I'd ridden a donkey on the beach once, aged five, so I was an expert rider, really. That's what I told Mr Hillgate, anyway. Even better, Brian was grey, which isn't quite silver, but it's similar.

Everything was perfect.

"OK then," said Mr Hillgate down the phone. "There's just one thing I should probably mention—"

Just then, I heard the timer go off for my cake. "Gotta run!" I said down the phone.

"Thanks so much and see you at the weekend!" I ended the call. Whatever it was, he could tell me on Saturday. It wouldn't be that important anyway – it was probably just to remind me that mucking out stables was hard work and to bring old shoes that I didn't mind getting ruined.

I hummed happily to myself as I strolled back through to the kitchen and pulled out two perfect cakes from the oven. Both had risen well and looked really good. Now I just had to let them cool before sandwiching them with jam and cream and topping the whole thing with icing and chocolate sprinkles.

"You seem happy," Henry muttered, as he finished laying out some goat's cheese tartlets on a plate. I had to admit, they looked pretty professional.

"Everything is just *so* perfect," I told him.

"Looking forward to your hummus!" he said, taking his platter of tartlets and heading out towards the living room.

I froze in horror. The hummus! I'd forgotten all about it and the guests were due in about ten minutes. But, OK! The horse was sorted, the cake was going to be delicious ... I could do this too! I hurried back to the computer and searched for a hummus recipe. I would need chickpeas, tahini, some garlic, lemon juice, various spices and seasoning. I briefly scanned the recipe, and it seemed you basically had to blend all the ingredients together into a smooth paste. Simple!

Back in the kitchen, I hunted through the cupboards for the things I needed. I found a tin of chickpeas, cracked it open, and poured the entire contents into the blender. Next, I needed tahini. This was a paste made from sesame seeds, but I couldn't find any anywhere. In fact, the only paste of any sort I could find was a pot of Thai curry paste.

I mean ... it was a paste, and it began with the letter 't' so it was partly what I needed. I checked the label on the back, and joy of joys! The label read: *may contain sesame*! What luck! It was a paste, beginning with the letter 't', which may have some sesame in it! Due to the doubts about how much sesame it actually had, I put in a huge dollop then added another two dollops for luck. Hopefully, between the three dollops, there would be a bit of sesame so that would be fine. Next, I added some lemon juice – or technically some lemon *squash*, due to a lack of actual lemons, then threw in the spices. I couldn't remember what the recipe said exactly, and the doorbell had just gone, so there wasn't time to check.

I whacked in some chilli, Chinese five spice, cloves and jerk seasoning. My thinking was that would cover most of the spices in existence, and some of them would be bound to be right. Now just to blend …

"Ah, Max!" Mum said, walking in. She was dressed in a beautiful, flowing dress, with a pretty flower pattern on it.

Honestly, even I had to admit she looked OK. She'd had her hair done, she had some nice shoes on, and she smelled of roses. "The first guests have just arrived," she said. "So, do you want to bring your hummus through?"

"Two seconds!" I said. "And, by the way, Mum, you look absolutely—"

I turned on the blender, and I'm not sure how it happened, but the lid must somehow have been a bit loose, because as the motor roared into life the contents of the jug rose up like a volcano and exploded out of the top, violently splattering all over me, the entire kitchen, and also … my mum.

I turned the blender off and slowly turned to see sloppy hummus dripping down Mum's face. Her whole dress was covered in hummus. And she smelled … well, she didn't smell of roses anymore, put it that way.

Her face was frozen. I couldn't quite place her expression.

Shock?

Horror?

I attempted a smile.

"You look absolutely ... beautiful," I told her.

4 Return of the Hummus

While Mum had a shower upstairs, I scraped the hummus off the walls and floor and put what I could salvage into a small bowl. When I walked through to the living room, everyone looked at me weirdly. To be fair, I was covered in hummus, but they should know it's rude to stare.

"This is Max," Adamma told everyone. "He's also been making food for tonight!"

Everyone glanced at me, and then at the small bowl of hummus I was holding. I picked some hairs out of it and held the bowl out for people to eat.

But nobody came forward.

"Isn't there anything to dip in it?" Henry eventually asked.

Oh dear. I'd forgotten that an important part of the whole dip experience was to have something to dip into … the dip.

Henry seemed to be smirking. I couldn't let him win this!

"Of course!" I said, lying. "I'll be one moment!"

I put the bowl on the table and hurried back through to the kitchen to find something to dip. I hunted through the cupboards and came across a packet of Jammie Dodger biscuits. They weren't ideal, but they'd have to do. Perhaps it would be an exciting taste experience? What else? I looked through the fridge, hoping to find a carrot I could chop into batons, but there was only some melon and an onion. I grabbed them anyway, quickly cut the onion into slices and melon into chunks, left the Jammie Dodgers as they were (who wants half a biscuit?), put everything on a plate, and went back to the living room.

"Help yourselves!" I announced, putting the plate down next to the bowl of hummus.

Henry glanced at my offering. "After you!" he said.

Everyone was staring at me, and nobody looked like they were going to try the hummus first. Fine! I would then. I grabbed a Jammie Dodger, scooped a nice big dollop of hummus onto it, and shoved the whole thing in my mouth.

The first thing that hit me was the sour, bitter, taste — like old fish. The second was the intense, burning heat.

I tried chewing and swallowing but it was like my body wouldn't cooperate. The sensible part of my brain was telling me to spit the repulsive food out. But another part of it was reminding me that Henry was watching all this, and I couldn't fail in front of him, our mums, and all their friends.

"You OK there?" Henry smirked.

I gave him a thumbs up. "Mmmmm!" I said, finally swallowing. "Oh my goodness! That was *so* tasty! Yummy-yum-yum-yumzies!"

"You'll be wanting another scoop then!" Henry said, smiling at me.

"I don't want to be greedy," I replied.

"Not at all," Henry said. "You've only had one little scoop of hummus. Have some more ... *if you like it so much!*"

Everyone was still staring at me.

"OK!" I said, finally. "Don't mind if I do!"

I took a slice of onion (big mistake) and another huge scoop of hummus (bigger mistake).

The strong, sharp taste of raw onion made me wince in pain. But I tried to smile, like this was enjoyable.

I slowly chewed as the mixture turned into a sort of thick, oniony concrete in my mouth ... I couldn't swallow it down, no matter how hard I tried ... Oh my goodness ... how had I messed up so badly?

Sweat beaded on my forehead as I kept on chewing, while the heat of everyone's eyes was still on me.

I gagged, then my vision started blurring ... that wasn't normal ... my stomach growled, then churned ... I knew that feeling ... I knew it meant I had about thirty seconds to get to the bathroom ...

I fled the living room and careered up the stairs, dizzy and hot, as the spicy bile bubbled away somewhere inside me.

It would have been fine had Mum not been coming out of her bedroom in her new outfit at the exact moment I was trying to reach the toilet. We collided. And the impact was the final straw.

For the second time that night, Mum was covered in hummus.

5 Mmm ... Chocolate Cake!

After Mum had got changed for the second time, we both made it downstairs and tried to enjoy the evening. Adamma had created a really cool playlist, people were chatting and laughing, and, really annoyingly, all of Henry's goat's cheese tartlets had been eaten. Everyone was saying things like:

"They were so delicious!" And ...

"You must give me the recipe!" And ...

"You're such a talented chef, Henry!"

And then they would look at me with sadness in their eyes, and say things like ...

"Never mind!" And ...

"We all have different talents!" And ...

"It's a shame about ruining *two* of your mum's best outfits!"

Two things were for sure. I was never making hummus again (it was now in the bin) and the evening wasn't over yet!

Henry was swanning around, lapping up all the praise and acting like butter wouldn't melt in his mouth, but I still had my ace card. The chocolate cake! Unlike hummus, I'd made the chocolate cake loads of times. I knew the recipe inside out, and I knew it always went down a storm. Once everyone tried the cake it would be me everyone loved, and Mum and Adamma would realise that I was the golden boy, not Henry.

While everyone else was dancing to a song called 'YMCA' I disappeared back to the kitchen to put the finishing touches to the cake. The two halves fell easily out of the cool tins and seemed to have the perfect spongy texture. Great! This was going to be my best cake ever!

First, I spread a thick layer of cherry jam all over one half, then topped that with a layer of freshly whipped cream. I sandwiched the halves together and then drizzled chocolate icing all over it. The silky, shiny sweet goodness enveloped the whole cake. *Yum*.

I took a step back to admire it. *Yes*. This was perfect. It just needed a couple more things: first, I dusted the top and sides with chocolate sprinkles, then I added a few whole cherries around the top. Finally, with white icing I wrote the words:

For my lovely mums, from Max

I heard the music stop in the living room and everyone clap their dance efforts. This was my moment! The crowning glory of the whole evening. I lifted the cake and carried it through. As soon as I arrived in the living room a hushed and respectful silence descended, and people parted to clear my path to the table. I walked slowly and purposefully, one foot in front of the other, like I was delivering a crown to a king.

"That looks amazing!" a woman said.

"What a beautiful cake!" said another.

"That kid can bake!" said a man in a fancy shirt.

Oh yeah! This was going to be my moment.

I placed the cake gently down on the table, as Mum appeared behind me with a knife and a stack of plates. "Oh, Max! What a lovely cake and what beautiful words iced on top of it!" she said.

"It's an *honour* to bake this cake," I said, glancing at Henry, who looked furious at all the attention I was getting.

Mum cut the cake into slices, the knife easily slipping through the moist, tender sponge. She handed the slices around on the plates. "Well, everyone!" she said. "Thank you for being here to celebrate tonight, thank you to Henry for the lovely goat's cheese tartlets, and a big thank you to Max for this splendid cake! It looks delicious, so let's tuck in!"

With that, she took a huge bite.

I watched, smiling, as everyone else took huge bites too.

Moments later, everyone had strange looks on their faces. I guess they'd just never tasted a chocolate cake as amazing as this before!

The man in the fancy shirt made a weird sound. A sort of strangled squeak. I guess he'd just never experienced a cake as divine as this ever in his life!

Mum's face had gone very pale. I suppose it must have been the shock at how tasty the cake was.

Adamma ... was crying? She literally had tears running down her cheeks! Oh my! She was crying because the cake was so beautiful! It had to be!

Just as I was ready to bask in all the applause and compliments, everyone started heaving and screaming and gasping for air.

"Gahhhhhh!" someone groaned.

"My mouth!" said another.

"What's in this?!" Adamma gasped. "Get water!"

"My mouth! My mouth!" Mum spluttered.

What was going on?

As everyone was falling about, gagging and retching, I took a small bite of my slice. Hm. It seemed perfectly ...

Gahhhhhhh!

I almost threw up again. Oh no. Oh *heck*. The cake just tasted of salt. I knew immediately what had happened.

I'd been so distracted thinking about how to get a horse that I hadn't been paying attention when I was measuring out the ingredients earlier. Salt can look a lot like sugar when you just glance at it. I'd put two hundred grammes of salt in this! It was a salt cake! And it was basically poison.

I spat the cake onto the plate and ran to the kitchen. We needed water. More than water, we needed something to take the salt-taste away! The first thing I saw was the bottle of passion-fruit fizz I'd bought from the supermarket. Perfect! And maybe it would be enough to make up for the cake, since the fizz had won several awards for tasting fabulous. I grabbed the bottle and ran back through to the living room. "Don't panic!" I shouted. "A quick glug of this beauty and we'll all be fine and dandy!"

I ripped off the silver foil that covered the cork. And then I'm not sure what happened, but looking back, I think me running with the bottle must have stirred up all the bubbles a bit too much, because WITH NO WARNING WHATSOEVER the cork suddenly fired off the end of the bottle like a bullet.

It hit the wall, broke a mirror, ricocheted off, and hit Adamma right in the face.

"OWWWWWWWW!" she howled, clutching her cheek and falling to the floor.

Ten minutes later, Mum was helping Adamma into the car to take her to A&E, while the guests downed pints of water before heading home to lie down and recover from their ordeal. Henry turned to me. "Well, Max," he said. "You've covered your own mum in the weirdest hummus ever made, *twice*, given everyone salt poisoning, and sent my mum to hospital after firing a cork at her actual face. *Congratulations.*"

I sighed and sunk down onto the sofa.

I was the worst pageboy the world had ever seen.

6 Another Fine Mess!

I sat next to Mum in the A&E waiting area with my head in my hands while Adamma was being treated in a cubicle. Henry was with her, and I was glad. The last thing I needed right then was him gloating about how perfect he was and how useless I was.

Plus, I'd made a decision and I didn't want Henry to be here when I told Mum.

"I think it's best if I pull out of being a pageboy," I muttered.

"Why, Max?" Mum replied.

I sighed and sat up, looking her straight in the eyes. "Because it's obvious I'm going to ruin your wedding. I've already ruined your hen night; I might have killed your wife-to-be — we simply don't know yet. How much more damage do you want me to do?"

Mum chuckled. "I'm pretty sure Adamma's going to be OK, Max."

I shrugged. "I really wanted to prove to everyone how good I was."

Mum turned to me. "What's this really about, Max? What's going on here?"

I chewed my lip, deep in thought. I didn't want to admit that I was worried about Henry taking my place. I felt embarrassed telling her that I thought she might prefer Henry to me, and I was about to be relegated to 'least favourite son' in the new family set-up and he'd get to choose the biscuits. Besides, I knew what she would say. She'd tell me I was being silly, that of course that wasn't the case, and she'd trot out some line about 'loving us both equally'.

Except, why would she?

Why would she still love me when Henry was the one who could cook, and write poetry, and say all the right things at exactly the right time?

I was an embarrassing mess who couldn't get anything right.

And Henry was basically perfect.

I sighed. "Nothing's going on," I told her. "Everything's fine. I just really wanted you to have the best wedding."

"The wedding's going to be a day to remember!" Mum said, smiling. "And I can't wait to see you come down that aisle with the ring, dressed as Cupid, on horseback!"

"Mm," I said, doubtfully. "Same."

Just then, Henry appeared from around the corner. "Mum's fine!" he said. "There wasn't any major damage, just a bit of swelling and bruising, but the doctors think it'll have gone down by the wedding day."

I sighed with relief.

"You can go and see her," Henry told my mum. "I'll wait here with Max and keep him out of trouble."

I gave Henry serious side-eye while Mum headed off to see Adamma. He flopped down onto a plastic chair next to me. "Look," he said, "considering what's happened, do you really think it's a good idea to come down the aisle on horseback?"

I gritted my teeth. I knew exactly what his game was! He wanted me to ditch my plans so I wouldn't overshadow him! It was so obvious. I mean, sure, he was probably right — all the evidence suggested it was a terrible idea that would end in tragedy — but that wasn't why he was suggesting it.

"Worried my entrance with the ring is going to be better than yours?" I said.

Henry smirked. I hated it when he smirked like that. It was always like he had extra tricks up his sleeve that I knew nothing about. "I'm not at all worried," he said.

"Well, you should be," I huffed. "Because my entrance is going to be *fabulous*."

"I'm sure it will be!" Henry chirped.

"You'd better believe it!"

"But ..." he continued, "my entrance is going to be ... *spectacular*!"

My breath caught. What had he got planned? How could it possibly be better than arriving on a massive horse? (Even if the horse was technically a donkey.)

"Worried?" he said, smiling.

"No."

"Want to know what I've got planned?"

"Not really."

Henry chuckled. "Sure, sure. Well, I'll tell you anyway. Picture the scene!" He swept his hands out in front of himself, painting the image.

"The music is playing, our mums are waiting for the rings to arrive ... the doors open at the back and you plod down the aisle on the back of some pony, but wait! What's that in the *actual sky*?! Is it a bird? Is it a plane? No! It's me! Henry! Being lowered from the ceiling on wires! I'll look like an actual angel! Everyone gasps! People weep with joy! All eyes will be on me – Cupid himself, appearing from the heavens!" He shook his head, like the whole thing was just too beautiful to even imagine. "My uncle runs a company that does special effects for stage shows – they're the people who make Peter Pan fly, and magic carpets, and so on. He's agreed to do me a favour."

I took a deep breath.

"Yep!" Henry continued. "It's going to be *big*. And, I thank you, actually."

"Do you?" I muttered.

"I do! Because if you hadn't mentioned arriving on the horse, I would never have thought about what I could do to make an even bigger gesture for our mums' big day."

"Great," I said, wishing I'd never mentioned the horse thing.

"Word of advice about the pony," Henry said.

"It's a *horse*."

"Is it though?" Henry said. "Let's face it, knowing you it'll probably turn out to be a cow or a camel or something. But whatever it is, make sure it goes to the toilet before coming into the hall." He leaned into me. "Nobody wants an accident at a wedding!"

A prickle of fear ran through me. It was a good point. Animals didn't tend to be fussy about where they went to the toilet, so how was I going to manage that situation?

Henry clapped his hands together. "Right! I'm peckish so I'm going to the vending machine. I fancy a chocolate bar!"

"Hope you don't choke on it," I muttered.

"Since *you* didn't make it, I'm confident I'll be fine!" Henry said, winking at me.

I stifled a scream. So far, Henry had won every single battle. He even had better comebacks than me. His banter was first class. Somehow, I had to make my arrival with the rings the best thing the world had ever seen. It needed to be so amazing, everyone would be looking at *me* and not at Henry, descending from the actual sky.

I shook my head. How had I got into this ridiculous mess?

7 Yay for Uncle Charlie!

It was the big day — the day of the wedding — a day of love and happiness and precious memories ... and also the day of me proving to everyone just how brilliant I was! *Hopefully*. Mum was getting ready at home and had a team of people fussing around her upstairs, helping with hair and make-up. Adamma was over at her house with Henry and was doubtless doing the same. All morning various phones were ringing with people wanting to confirm flower arrangements and times to serve food at the reception party afterwards, while an endless stream of people came to the front door with bouquets and chocolates and things like that. Someone even came along with a sewing machine, to make last-minute alterations to Mum's dress.

All of this was a massive distraction, because I had things I needed to arrange myself.

Despite my pleas, Mum had refused to allow me to have a bow and arrow as Cupid.

"But why not?" I had said to Mum. "Imagine it! I enter on horseback, shooting arrows at all the mourners!"

"They're guests, not 'mourners', Max!" Mum replied. "It isn't a funeral! But it might be if you start shooting arrows at everyone!"

I slapped my forehead. "Not *actual* arrows with sharp points, Mum!" I howled. "Toy arrows, with little notes attached to them that say things like, 'The guy two rows behind really likes you!' I'll be literally bringing people together in love and romance!"

Mum frowned at me. "That sounds like a recipe for disaster. A lot of folks who are coming already have partners – that'll just cause arguments and be really awkward for everyone. *No*. It's not happening."

"But, Mum!"

"*No.*"

So, that was that. I was just going to have to make the most of entering on horseback. Luckily, I had managed to add some extra magic to the whole affair.

A dry-ice machine!

These were the sorts of things you often saw at big pop concerts and they created huge amounts of billowing mist all over the floor.

With the machine turned on, I would then emerge, on my majestic silver horse, through the mist, to the astonishment of all the mourners. I mean, *guests.* The mist would cover the entire lower part of the room, meaning it would look like the horse and I were floating through the air.

Surely everyone would be looking at that, rather than Henry dangling from a rope?

I'd persuaded my Uncle Charlie to lend me the dry-ice machine. Uncle Charlie was Mum's brother, and he was coming up from London for the wedding. He was very loud and very flamboyant. He also ran a mobile disco business, which is why he had a dry-ice machine.

He told me the machine was a bit old and temperamental. I told him that was OK, so was my mum, and I coped with her just fine!

Uncle Charlie laughed at that.

At least someone appreciates me.

While I waited for Uncle Charlie to arrive, I changed into my Cupid outfit. I didn't have high hopes for the costume, but after slipping on the toga, and with the accompanying silver socks, silver glitter boots, feathered wings, and the garland of silver spray-painted roses around my head, I looked …

Well, I looked ridiculous, let's be honest.

But if I had to look ridiculous, I just hoped I was going to look less ridiculous than Henry. I puffed my chest out. I tried to look proud. Sometimes you just have to fake it to make it.

At 11am Uncle Charlie arrived to take me to the wedding venue so I could get ready. "Max!" he trilled, as I opened the door. "Let's rock and roll!"

"Make sure he doesn't get into any trouble!" Mum shouted down the stairs.

"I'll be fine, Mum!" I replied.

"I meant Uncle Charlie!" she told me. "You need to make sure *he* doesn't get into any trouble, Max!"

I shook my head. Mum thought Uncle Charlie was 'irresponsible', but I liked him. He was always good fun and would often suggest doing things that Mum would never let me do. Like the time he took me abseiling. And one occasion when we tried paragliding. OK, sure, we did once get stuck on the top of a mountain in a raging storm, with no coats, in just our flip-flops, and have to be rescued by a helicopter, but that could happen to anyone.

Uncle Charlie was dressed in a bright pink suit with a black shirt and matching pink bow tie. On his head was a black hat with a pink feather in it. At least someone else looked as wild as I did.

"Loving the glitter boots!" Uncle Charlie grinned, as I got into his car.

The car in question was a two-seater sports car with a folded down roof and a big engine. Mum said Uncle Charlie had been 'irresponsible' buying the car, because he often had no money and should really be saving up for more important things. However, there was no denying the car was cool. And as we sped towards the wedding venue, I had to admit, I felt good. I felt like everything might just work out for me.

The wedding venue was called Beaumont Castle and it stood in acres and acres of gardens. Lush green lawns surrounded the castle, with a grand gravel driveway up to the entrance, which was flanked with tall oak trees, with colourful flowerbeds beyond. The castle itself was really old, but it had been renovated, and the wedding was taking place in the Great Hall, which was a huge space, with a high, vaulted ceiling, and stained-glass windows.

That was all very nice, but my smile quickly dropped when I spied the creature standing next to Mr Hillgate by the entrance.

He had two gigantic front teeth sticking out of his mouth in different directions.

He had several bald patches on his back.

He had flies swarming around his rear end.

And I couldn't be one hundred per cent sure if it was him, or a sewer was blocked, but *the stench*!

I've never smelled anything so bad in my life!

This couldn't be Brian ... could it?

8 Stinking Donkey

I clambered out of the car and strode over to Mr Hillgate. "I'm here to collect Brian," I said. I glanced at the creature standing next to him who was now drooling. "Where is he?" I asked, hopefully.

Mr Hillgate indicated the creature, and my heart sank. "Really?" I said. And then I gagged because of the smell. "Why does he stink like that?"

"Stink? What stink?" Mr Hillgate replied, breathing in deeply. "I can't smell anything!"

I wrinkled my nose. Mr Hillgate had obviously got used to the stench. Maybe I could borrow some of Uncle Charlie's aftershave and give Brian a spritz?

"OK, well, how do I get on him?" I asked.

Mr Hillgate shook his head. "No, you can't ride him. I tried to warn you about that on the phone, but you said you had to go. He's recovering from a hip operation, you see. I'd have explained, if you'd given me the chance!"

I glared at Mr Hillgate, panic rising in my chest. "But riding him was the whole point!" I squealed.

With that, Brian started bucking about, also squealing. Mr Hillgate tried to soothe him by rubbing his head while keeping a tight hold on his harness. "He also doesn't like loud noises," Mr Hillgate told me, when Brian was calm again. "So keep your voice down!"

I rolled my eyes.

"Also," Mr Hillgate added, "he's got a real passion for flowers. If he smells flowers, he'll be off! He'll hunt them down and be eating them before you know it!"

"Flowers?!" I hissed, remembering to keep my voice down. "You do know this is a wedding? There will be flowers everywhere!"

"Oh dear," said Mr Hillgate. "Well, just keep a tight hold of him as you walk down the aisle. I'm sure it'll be fine."

I took a deep breath. Cupid leading a stinking, bald, buck-toothed donkey down the aisle. What kind of weird, messed-up myth was I going to be presenting here?

Uncle Charlie strode up to join us, having parked his car. He was carrying what I presumed was the dry-ice machine. "Here it is!" Uncle Charlie said, holding the machine up. "The Fog Max 3000! They use this for all

the big concerts! Pumps out fog like you've never seen!"

"I was after more of a *mist*," I said. "I want everyone to be able to see me."

Uncle Charlie shrugged. "So, should I set the dial to maximum or minimum?"

"Minimum!" I said.

With that, Brian started bucking about again.

"Easy, lad! Easy!" Mr Hillgate cooed. "You *must* keep your voice down!"

"I didn't even shout," I said. "That was normal volume!"

"He's *very* sensitive!" Mr Hillgate told me.

"The dial needs to be at minimum!" I whispered to Uncle Charlie.

"I know, I was just winding you up!" Uncle Charlie said, grinning. "You need to chill out!"

"It's a very big day for me!" I told him.

"And you'll ace it!" he replied.

I really hoped he was right. I left Uncle Charlie to chat with Mr Hillgate and walked through the huge, heavy wooden doors into the Great Hall. At the far end, Henry was rehearsing flying in as Cupid. They'd rigged up some scaffolding and Henry was wearing a harness, attached to various wires. It looked a bit dangerous, if you asked me, but I guess his uncle knew what he was doing – as long as he was nothing like my uncle!

Right on cue, Uncle Charlie walked in behind me, saw Henry's uncle and shouted, "Jamal?!"

Henry's uncle looked up from where he was adjusting Henry's harness, saw my uncle, and his face broke into a wide smile. "Charlie! Long time, no see!"

With that, both our uncles ran towards each other down the aisle, like long-lost relatives, embraced, and did a complicated handshake, accompanied by both of them making the noise of a parakeet, for some reason.

They were obviously old mates.

Henry glared at me, then turned and walked through a wooden door at the side, so he wouldn't be seen before his entrance. I needed to hide too, so the surprise wouldn't be ruined. I hurried back outside, where Mr Hillgate handed me Brian's rope. "Good luck, kid!" he said. "I'm heading off for my lunch, but I'll come and collect Brian afterwards."

I couldn't quite place the feeling, but it was a bit like when you knew you had a big test in school, and you hadn't done enough preparation. I felt a bit jittery, and like nothing was quite as it should be. But it was too late now. The first wedding guests were starting to arrive, and that meant Mum and Adamma wouldn't be far behind. I tied Brian up to a nearby tree, and went to wait around the corner, out of sight.

I had to wait ages while all the guests arrived, but eventually they all seemed to be inside. Five minutes later, I poked my head around the corner and watched as Mum arrived in one car, with Adamma just behind in another. Mum was going to walk down the aisle first and Adamma would follow. There would then be lots of speaking, and a song, and then it would be time for the rings — which was mine and Henry's bit.

Mum stepped out of the car, and I couldn't help but smile. She looked absolutely beautiful. Her hair was in ringlets, and she looked happy and sparkling. She was wearing an ivory dress, quite simple, not one of those huge puffy ones, just stylish and sophisticated. Adamma looked just as stunning — also in ivory, but with more lace. On their feet, they both wore matching black boots — which Mum told me was a little bit of fun to make the wedding seem less formal. I liked it. I think it's great when people do something a bit different and don't just follow the crowd. I guess it was just another way they wanted this day to be memorable.

Mum gave me a thumbs up, so I gave one back, and then the ceremony started. As music began playing from inside, Mum headed in first, followed by Adamma. I hovered just outside, watching, as they took their places at the front with the celebrant — that's the posh

name for the lady who was going to marry them. After some talking, and some more talking, and some kind of joke the celebrant made that everyone laughed at, there was a song, and that was my cue to get ready.

I untied Brian and led him to the door of the Great Hall.

I adjusted the wings that were attached to my back.

And I took a deep breath.

At the front, the celebrant said, "And now it's time for the arrival of the rings!"

Music started playing. Mist started filling the air. And I walked forwards …

9 A Wedding to Remember!

The Great Hall was full. Guests were sitting on chairs either side of the aisle, with huge bouquets of flowers along the walls. At least the flowers weren't anywhere near me and Brian, so I hoped he wouldn't be tempted. The room was lit by big candles, casting everything in a beautiful, warm glow.

Everyone gasped as a gentle mist started billowing down the aisle. It was all very lovely and very magical. Almost like a fairy tale.

As I walked forwards with Brian, I could see Henry, in the air up ahead, slowly being lowered down. The guests weren't sure where to look. Some were looking at me, as I pulled a stinking donkey behind me; some were staring at Henry, clearly amazed at how he was flying in with the ring. But if I was worried about Henry getting more attention, I didn't need to be for long.

"What's that terrible smell?" one woman said, looking at me and Brian.

"I promise, it's not me!" I mouthed back to her.

The woman frowned and wafted several flies away from her face.

As we passed each row, people choked and gagged, and held their noses. One man looked like he might faint.

We were about halfway down the aisle when we passed a woman with a massive hat. I realised just too late that it had several flowers sticking out of it. I tried to walk a bit more quickly with Brian, but nothing could stop his smelling superpower. He suddenly jerked his head to the right and stuffed his snout into the woman's hat. He gobbled the flowers, and then he licked her face for good measure.

It was at this point the woman screamed. Which was kind of understandable, but also *really bad*.

Brian was startled by the loud noise, so he immediately went haywire. Bucking about, he careered down the aisle, breaking loose from the rope I was holding.

"NOOOOO!" I screamed. But, of course, that only made things worse.

As Brian continued his rampage through the Great Hall, the fog from the machine was getting thicker. I could just about make out Uncle Charlie, who was filming all the chaos on his phone, when he should have been making sure the Fog Max 3000 was set to minimum. Based on the fact the entire Great Hall was thick with smog at this point, I would say it was set to maximum and Uncle Charlie was indeed 'irresponsible', just like Mum had warned me.

Somewhere, a huge bouquet of flowers crashed over, then another. Someone screamed, someone else cried, "HELP!" And, I don't know how it happened, but the wires holding Henry must have got tangled, or maybe something snapped, or maybe the person operating them was blinded by all the fog. At any rate, the next thing I knew, poor Henry suddenly dropped down about two metres, before dangling dangerously mid-air.

"Help!" he cried. "Help! I'm going to fall!"

My eyes widened. Henry might not have been my favourite person right then, but I didn't want him to come to any harm! There was no time to lose. I wasn't quite sure what I was going to do, but I ran towards him. Unfortunately, due to all the fog, I couldn't see, so I tripped over a step and face-planted on the floor right under him, at the exact moment the cable snapped, and Henry dropped down, landing right on top of me as I broke his fall.

"Oof!" I said, completely winded.

"Oof!" Henry said.

"Fire!" someone else shouted.

I twisted around and just about made out Brian, who had knocked over a huge candle, which had set light to some rainbow-coloured bunting.

Argh! How much worse could this get?!

I wriggled out from under Henry, managed to make out the shape of a fire extinguisher through the haze and grabbed it. I pulled out the pin, aimed the hose and sprayed foam all over the flames ... but it was so powerful!

The hose took on a life of its own, and I somehow managed to also cover the guests, and the entire Great Hall.

People screamed. Smoke billowed. I sprayed until the extinguisher was empty.

As the fog cleared, there was a shocked silence.

Everyone was coated, head to toe, in foam.

The Great Hall was wrecked.

I slowly turned to look at Mum and Adamma.

They were standing there, foam dripping off them, dresses ruined, looking shocked.

I'd really done it now. I was going to be grounded forever.

And then ... Mum snorted.

And Adamma giggled.

Then Mum laughed.

And Adamma hooted.

Before I knew it, everyone was in hysterics!

"We wanted a wedding to remember!" Mum laughed. "And we certainly got one!"

10 Game on!

Later that afternoon we were all enjoying the reception party in a barn in the grounds of the castle. Music was playing, people were dancing, and there was loads of lovely food — and don't worry, I hadn't made any of it!

"Thank you for saving my life," Henry said, walking up to me. He held out a hand. "Friends?"

I shook it. "Friends."

Mum and Adamma came over to join us. "Have you two made up?" Adamma asked.

"Yeah," I chuckled. "I guess we got a bit too competitive, trying to make the wedding fun for you both, but it's all good now."

"I'm glad!" Mum said. "Because we have exciting news!" My eyes widened.

"We've found the perfect house for us all to live in together!" Adamma said.

"It's in the country, so I can keep a horse!" Mum added.

"Like I've always wanted!"

"Oh, cool!" I replied.

"Yeah, that sounds good!" Henry added.

Mum smiled. "Now, you'll both get a bedroom each, but one of them is bigger than the other and has its own bathroom, so Adamma and I thought a fair way of deciding who gets the best room would be a friendly little competition!"

My heart skipped a beat.

"We're going to assign you each a room downstairs to design!" Adamma said. "You get to choose the theme, decor, colour scheme and furniture. We'll get Uncle Charlie and Uncle Jamal to judge the designs without telling them which of you did which one, and the winner gets first choice of bedroom!"

"May the bedroom wars commence!" Mum said, grinning.

I looked at Henry.

Henry looked at me.

His eyes narrowed.

So did mine.

Oh yeah. It was *game on*!

Now answer the questions ...

1 Where did Max's mum meet Adamma?

2 Why did Max's mum send him to his room after he told the joke on page 12?

3 Max found a donkey sanctuary so that he could borrow a donkey. What does 'sanctuary' mean?

4 What happened when the people at the hen party ate the cake that Max had made?

5 After Max and Henry have planned their grand entrances to the wedding, what did you think would happen?

6 Mum called Uncle Charlie 'irresponsible' – what does this mean?

7 How did Max feel about Henry at the start of the story compared to the end?

8 Have you ever been to a wedding? Did anything funny, strange or surprising happen?